Introduction

This book is about an amazing period of British history, when for the first time an Englishman sailed around the world, North America was discovered, printed books appeared and Spain tried to invade England.

Today it is called the Tudor period, which started with Henry Tudor in 1485 and ended with the death of Queen Elizabeth I in 1603. It was the end of the Middle Ages and the start of the Renaissance in Europe, which saw a revival of Greek and Roman art and learning, new ideas and philosophies. It all spread quickly because of printing, world expansion and the Protestant Reformation, when the church in England split from Rome.

Some of the most colourful and exciting kings and queens reigned during this time. This book will tell you all about their interesting lives, as well as what life was like for ordinary people.

Contents

Written & illustrated by William Webb
Front cover illustration by Les Ives
Published by Colour Heroes Ltd © 2009
Print reference number 32409/06/09

The Tudor Dynasty

The House of Tudor probably started with 'Old King Cole', a Romano-British chieftain called Coel Hen Godebog, who ruled Colchester in the 4th century AD. The Tudors were also related to the Welsh hero Owain Glyndwr, who fought for Welsh independence in 1400.

The Wars of the Roses

Since the middle of the 15th century a civil war had been going on in England between the Houses of Lancaster and York. These two great noble families both had claims to the throne, because they were both descended from King Edward III. They were called the 'Wars of the Roses' because the symbol for Lancaster was a red rose and the Yorkist emblem was a white rose.

The Princes in the Tower

When King Edward IV died in 1483 he left two sons who were too young to rule. Edward decided that their Uncle Richard, Duke of Gloucester should be made 'Protector' and rule until Edward the eldest son and Prince of Wales, was old enough to rule. However, the Duke had other plans and his supporters put the two young Princes, Edward and his brother Richard, Duke of York, in the Tower of London. The Tower was used as a home as well as a prison and it was claimed that they were there for their protection. They were never heard of again. Some claim that the Duke of Gloucester had the boys murdered, so that he could become King. Others think that Henry Tudor, who also had a claim to the throne, had them killed.

Richard Duke of Gloucester Crowned King

Even while the two Princes were alive, their claim to the throne was rejected and Richard Duke of Gloucester was offered the crown. He was crowned King Richard III at Westminster Abbey in 1483. He was cruelly known as 'Crookback', probably because of some physical deformity. He was not very popular because people were suspicious of the Princes' deaths.

Skeletons Under the Stairs

The skeletons of two boys were discovered beneath a staircase in the Tower (right) during building repairs. Charles II had their remains put in Westminster Abbey, but even though they were the right ages, no one knows if they are definitely the two missing Princes.

He imprisoned many nobles who he suspected of plotting against him. He had a son, who only lived for a year and his Queen died not long afterwards at the age of 28 years. Without an heir to the throne, Richard made the Earl of Lincoln his successor.

Henry Tudor

The House of Lancaster saw this as an opportunity to press their claim to the throne. Their champion was Henry Tudor who had been living in exile in France. He gathered support and met King Richard at Bosworth Field in Leicestershire in 1485.

The Battle of Bosworth

Richard had 8,000 men against Henry's 3,000. However, during the battle Lord Stanley, Henry's stepfather, who had not decided which side he would fight on, helped Henry. His 3,000 men assured the Lancastrians victory. Richard fought bravely, but he was killed and the crown rolled off his head. Lord Stanley gave it to Henry who was officially crowned King Henry VII at Westminster Abbey on 30th October, 1485. Henry married Elizabeth of York, the daughter of Edward IV and the Yorkist heir to the throne, bringing the two houses together and ending the Wars of the Roses. It was the start of the reign of the Tudor monarchs.

Henry Secures his Throne

However, during his reign Henry still had to fight and defeat others who claimed to be heirs to the throne. Some claimed to be one of the princes from the Tower. Their claims were false, but were often backed by enemies of England, such as France and Scotland. To end these threats Henry married his daughters to the Kings of France and Scotland and his son Henry to a Spanish princess. He also limited the power of the English nobles by stopping them from getting too wealthy, banning the building of castles and by outlawing private armies.

The Battle of Bosworth

22nd August 1485

Archers were trained from boyhood to master the difficult pull of the longbow. They were well paid for their services and could fire 50 arrows off within a few minutes. At close range their arrows could pierce plate armour!

Handgunners using very primitive guns, mingled amongst the archers. The gun took a while to load and could only fire about one lead or pewter shot a minute.

Foot soldiers used their pole axes to pull knights off their saddles, or to smash the skulls of their opponents. By now knights often fought on foot and also used this weapon, to lunge at the enemy. They would aim for the face, or pull and twist the back of a soldier's knee, crippling him.

Knights fought on foot because their foot soldiers distrusted their ability to quickly flee the battle on their horses if things were going badly. So, they dismounted and often died with their men. Neither Henry or Richard III could trust their armies to fight for them. Richard III had to take hostages to make sure his commanders obeyed him!

Henry VIII

On the death of his father, Henry VII in 1509, Henry VIII was crowned King shortly before his 18th birthday. He already had a wife, the country was at peace and the Treasury was full. He was to become the most famous King of England.

The King with the 'X Factor'!

Henry VIII enjoyed a variety of pastimes and was a very talented young man. He loved hunting and jousting, dancing, illustrating, writing music and going to war! He let the Archbishop of York, Thomas Wolsey, run the country while he indulged himself. He was handsome and athletic, well educated, could speak several languages, including Latin and is said to have written the famous song 'Greensleeves'. He even fought and beat the French.

Things Start to go Wrong

However, after only ten years the Treasury was empty. Of six children born to him only one, Mary, survived. Henry desperately wanted a male heir. He wanted to divorce his wife, Catherine of Aragon, despite it being a largely happy marriage. In those days people did not divorce like they do now. Wolsey failed to persuade the Pope to allow the divorce, so he fell from Henry's favour. He lost his job as Lord Chancellor and was falsely accused of High Treason, or plotting against the King. He lost his riches, including the fabulous palace of Hampton Court, which the King had always wanted. Wolsey died on the way to London after being arrested.

Anne Boleyn and the Split from Rome

Before his divorce from Catherine, Henry had already been courting Anne Boleyn who became pregnant. They had a secret marriage in 1533 and his divorce was declared official by the new Archbishop of Canterbury, Thomas Cranmer. Henry no longer recognised the authority of the Roman Catholic Church in Rome, as they opposed the divorce. Now the English Parliament made the King the official head of the Church of England instead of the Pope.

1536 - A Busy Year!

Catherine of Aragon died and Henry and his new Queen unkindly celebrated her death by dressing in bright yellow, ordering a thanksgiving mass, feasting, dancing and jousting!

However, Ann only managed to produce a baby girl, Elizabeth. Henry accused her of unfaithfulness and treason and she was beheaded at the Tower of London. He then married one of Anne's maids of honour, Jane Seymour. In the same year Henry seized the opportunity he now had as head of the church to fill his empty treasury. His new chief advisor, Thomas Cromwell, came up with the idea of closing, or 'dissolving' the smaller monasteries and houses and selling the properties. In those days the church owned about a third of all the land in England and Wales and its annual income was three times that of the government. Over 500 religious houses were sold, or dismantled for cash and 7,000 monks, 2,000 nuns and 50,000 ordinary workers lost their livelihoods. Many of the poor lost vital charity and care.

Wife Number Four!

The following year Jane Seymour died after giving birth to a boy, Edward. Now, Thomas Cromwell arranged a marriage to a German princess, Anne of Cleves. Henry sent his court painter, the German Hans Holbein (see page 13), to paint her and her sister, so that he could choose the more beautiful of the two. When he finally met his choice, he was so displeased that even though he married Anne he later divorced her and had Cromwell executed! Holbein kept his job though! The King remained good friends with Anne and gave her two houses to live in.

Wives Five and Six!

His next wife was the pretty Catherine Howard. She was 15, he was 49, fat, unpleasant, prematurely old and suffering from syphilis. Catherine unwisely continued some previous love affairs and was found out and beheaded at the Tower. Finally, Henry married a woman who had been widowed twice, Catherine Parr. A clever woman and the first Protestant Queen, she survived attempts to remove her by Catholics. Henry died in 1547 leaving three heirs, Mary, Elizabeth and Edward. Catherine married again the same year, but died giving birth to a baby girl.

Henry's Wives

2. Anne Boleyn
Anne was the mother of Elizabeth I. Certain men were accused of having affairs with Anne so the King could execute her. They were found guilty of treason, hung, cut down whilst still alive and disembowelled and quartered.

1. Catherine of Aragon
She was originally betrothed to Henry's older bother Arthur when she was just 2 years old! She eventually married Arthur at the age of 16, but then Arthur died.

3. Jane Seymour
Jane was the only one of Henry's wives to be buried with him in St George's Chapel at Windsor Castle. She bore him his only son, Edward.

Henry VIII
A portrait by Hans Holbein

6. Catherine Parr
She was responsible for educating and taking care of Edward, Mary and Elizabeth when Henry died, even though she was a similar age to Mary.

4. Anne of Cleves
Henry unkindly called her 'the Flunders mare'. Her face is not unattractive and it may be that Henry's real objection to her was to do with her personality.

5. Catherine Howard
Catherine Howard had been a lady in waiting to Anne of Cleves. Henry called her his 'rose without a thorn' and the 'very jewel of womanhood'.

Draw a portrait of a girl or boy in your class. Try to make the person look their best, so that they would be happy with their portrait. How closely do you think it looks like them? What does the person you drew think? What do other people in your class think?

Edward VI, Lady Jane & Bloody Mary!

Henry's children Edward, Elizabeth and Mary were all to reign over England, but none was to produce an heir to the throne. Edward was only nine when he became King and he lived for just six more years.

He was educated by the finest scholars in England and was brought up in the new Protestant faith, which was sweeping over Europe. Under his rule England became a Protestant country. Surrounded by adults most of his life, Edward was extremely clever, but he lacked a normal childhood. All of the learning did not help his poor health either. Although he survived measles and smallpox, he died of tuberculosis, complicated by his father's sickness, at the age of 15 years in 1553.

Lady Jane Grey

While Edward lay dying, his Protector, the Duke of Northumberland, persuaded him to name Lady Jane Grey his successor. Lady Jane was a great granddaughter of Henry VII. The Duke of Northumberland had already arranged for her to marry his own son! They did not want the Catholic princess Mary to become Queen, but wanted a Protestant on the throne. Lady Jane was proclaimed Queen at the age of fifteen, but she would not agree to Northumberland's son, Guildford Dudley becoming King. However, Mary's supporters rallied around her and after nine days Mary managed to arrest Northumberland, Guildford and Lady Jane. Mary became Queen in 1553 and a year later there was a Protestant uprising in Kent led by Sir Thomas Wyatt. It was stopped in London by Mary's soldiers, but she realised that as long as Lady Jane was still alive she was a threat. So, reluctantly she agreed that Northumberland, Guildford and Lady Jane should be beheaded at the Tower.

Unhappy Mary

Mary was very popular with the people, but her popularity was soon to disappear, because she was a Catholic and wanted England to return to her faith. She married the Catholic King of Spain, Philip II, to try to get an heir. His head appeared on English coins. The marriage was unpopular with the English nobles who feared they would lose the lands they had gained from the dissolution of the monasteries. Philip also dragged England into a war with France, but he lost England's last possession in France, the port of Calais. Mary never forgave herself for this loss. Philip stayed with Mary for a few months, but left her and returned to Spain. Even though Mary was in love with him, Philip did not like her and he complained of a horrible smell coming from her nose! Mary was not a healthy woman and like Edward had inherited her father's sickness, which stopped her from having children.

Bloody Mary!

After the Protestant uprising, Mary persecuted all of those who would not convert to Catholicism. Many fled the country, but about 300 were burned at the stake. This is how Mary received her nickname, 'Bloody Mary', though it has to be said that under her successor Elizabeth, just as many Catholics were put to death. Mary died broken hearted in 1558 at the age of 42 years.

Martyred for their Faith

On 16th October, 1555 Protestant bishops Ridley and Latimer were burned at the stake. Ridley's brother tied a bag of gunpowder to both of their necks. As a burning bundle of twigs was laid at the feet of Ridley, Latimer spoke his famous words, "Be of good comfort, Master Ridley, and play the man; we shall this day light such a candle. By God's grace, in England, as I trust shall never be put out." Latimer appeared to die swiftly and without too much pain, but Ridley's legs burned completely while his upper body remained untouched. He screamed for some wood to be removed, so that the flames would rise more quickly. Finally, a bystander pulled the wood from the fire and it flamed to his face, igniting the gunpowder. When he had died hundreds of bystanders looked on at the two motionless bodies and all that could be heard was weeping.

The Golden Age of Elizabeth

Elizabeth became one of England's greatest monarchs. She established a national church, maintained foreign alliances by hinting at marriage, defeated a Spanish invasion, increased England's power in the Americas and advanced the arts.

Elizabeth had a difficult childhood, having lost her mother at the age of three and her father Henry had wanted a boy. Although she accompanied her sister Mary to her coronation, she spent Mary's reign in the Tower and at Hatfield House under arrest. Fortunately, Henry's sickness had not affected her as it had affected Mary and Edward.

Like Father Like Daughter
Elizabeth was multi-talented like her father. She could speak five languages, was a gifted musician, a graceful dancer and a fine archer. She reigned for 45 years and was popular with the people who called her 'Good Queen Bess'. Although surrounded by male advisors, she was a strong and clever ruler who earned their love and respect. She was vain and loved to wear magnificent dresses, insisting that other women in court could only wear white and silver. As Elizabeth grew older she wore a big red wig and used lots of cosmetics. She could stir people with her speeches and powerful presence. Under her reign the Protestant faith was re-established, despite threats from successive Popes.

Many Admirers
The Queen remained unmarried throughout her life, but she had a series of lovers. They included the poet and explorer Sir Walter Raleigh, the Earl of Leicester and then later his stepson, the Earl of Essex. When Leicester died, Elizabeth was so upset that she locked herself in her room and only came out when worried staff broke the door down. Essex misjudged how much the Queen liked him and after a series of mistakes he was eventually executed in 1601.

Did You Know?
When Elizabeth died, she left over 3,000 dresses and head decorations.

Mary Queen of Scots
Elizabeth's cousin, Mary Stuart, became Queen of Scotland when she was a week old on the death of her father King James V of Scotland. She was brought up a Catholic in France and married the dauphin of France. When he became King in 1559 she became the Queen of France and she also had a claim to the English throne. Mary was beautiful and very clever and when her husband died she returned to Scotland. Mary was not popular in her strongly Protestant homeland and after two scandalous marriages she was forced to give up the throne to her baby son, James VI. She escaped capture and fled to England and begged Elizabeth for mercy. Mary was imprisoned, as she was a threat to the English throne and Elizabeth's advisors wanted Mary executed. Elizabeth refused to allow this until she was told that Mary had been involved in a plot to kill her. Even after Mary's execution in 1587, Elizabeth claimed she had never agreed to her cousin's death.

Protestant Persecution
The Pope declared that it wasn't a sin to kill Elizabeth, which was a fatal mistake. Elizabeth had been keen to allow both faiths to peacefully co-exist, but now Catholics were persecuted. Heavy fines were demanded from those who refused to give up Catholicism. Many priests went into hiding and in some houses special hiding places, or 'priest holes', were made for Catholic clergymen to hide.

The Travelling Queen
Queen Elizabeth made London her home, but during the summer her entire court travelled with her as far as Derby, Dover and Bristol. She made herself the guest of wealthy nobles who spent thousands of pounds entertaining her. She went riding, deer hunting, feasting and played games, but she also spent time mingling with local farmers and villagers. She died at the age of 69 and was succeeded by King James I, who was also James VI of Scotland.

Bloody Times

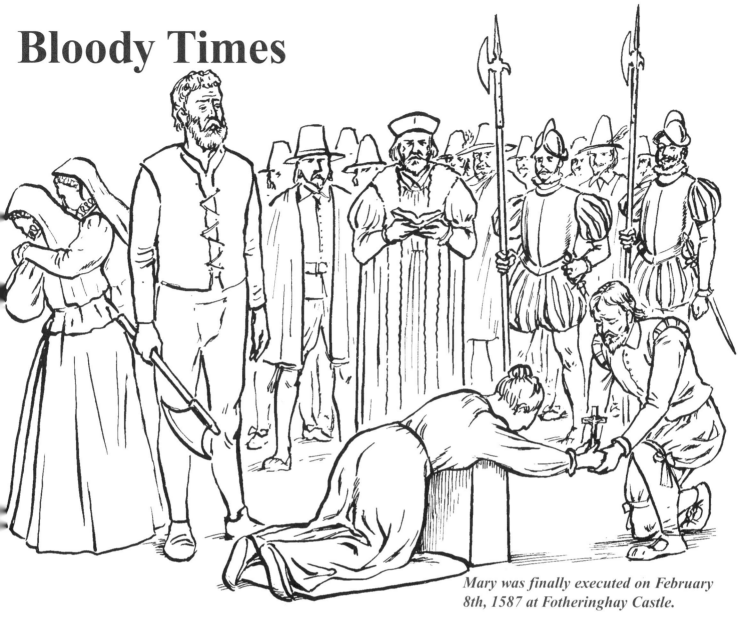

Mary was finally executed on February 8th, 1587 at Fotheringhay Castle.

Crime & Punishment

In the Tudor period there wasn't a police force to enforce the law. Constables were appointed to bring people to justice and the government created Justices of the Peace to hear cases brought before them. Justices of the Peace had to prevent riots, report anyone who did not attend church services and managed the building of poor houses, bridges, roads and jails.

Tudor punishments were harsh and included hanging, burning to death, torture, whipping, being put in stocks (right) where people could pelt you with rubbish, dunking in a river or being branded with a hot iron. Some criminals were humiliated by being locked in a cage in the centre of a busy market, in full view of the passers by.

The 'Ducking Stool' (see below) had been used since Saxon times and was usually reserved for women, such as 'scolds', butchers, bakers, apothecaries and brewers who cheated on measures, or sold bad food. The person had to sit in the chair after being wheeled through the town and was then 'ducked' into a river. This punishment continued until the early 19th century!

Some offences seem very odd. In 1573 several people were fined for wearing hats instead of caps! This was because Queen Elizabeth I had made the wearing of woollen caps compulsory on Sundays to encourage the wool trade!

The Armada

Philip II of Spain felt he had a claim to the English throne, as he had been married to Mary, Elizabeth's half-sister. Mary had died in 1558, but Philip II wanted to marry Elizabeth and restore England to the Catholic faith. Elizabeth refused to marry him and he was further angered by English support for his Dutch enemies. So, he started to build what he called an 'Invincible Armada', or fleet of ships to invade England.

Philip prepared for a huge invasion. He wanted to secure the English Channel with his fleet, so that an army of 19,500 men waiting in the Netherlands could cross to England. With the help of English Catholics and his 20,000 troops, plus 10,000 sailors on his ships, he felt he could remove Elizabeth from the English throne.

England Prepares for the Invasion

England already had a good fleet of ships and experienced sea captains. They had gained their expertise by robbing Spanish lands and ships in the Americas, men like Sir Francis Drake, John Hawkins and Martin Frobisher. The Queen had advanced warning of the invasion and prepared for it by organising troops on the coast.

Setbacks for Philip

Sir Francis Drake carried out a raid on the Spanish port of Cadiz where Spanish ships were being built. He caused great havoc and managed to burn large quantities of barrels, which would have been used to carry food and wine for the Spanish fleet. Due to the loss of the barrels, Philip had to reduce the size of the army he was sending. Many Spanish ships were damaged by storms even before they left Spanish waters. Despite warnings from his advisors, Philip pushed ahead with the invasion and chose the Duke of Medina Sidonia to command his fleet. The Duke tried to get out of it because he had no naval experience and he suffered from seasickness! If Philip was counting on the help of English Catholics, even they were against the Spanish invasion.

The Battle

By the time the two navies met, the Spanish had already been at sea for two weeks. Their ships were heavier because they had to carry provisions for two months and the sailors were more vulnerable to disease. The English fleet were supplied daily from the coast by smaller ships. They were now evenly matched. The first shots were fired on July 31st and two Spanish ships were disabled and Francis Drake captured one of them after dark. Fighting continued during the next few days, but without serious casualties. Eventually the Armada reached Calais, where it waited for news of its invasion army's arrival and took on fresh supplies. However, the army in the Netherlands was not ready to invade yet. At Calais, Drake launched an attack on the Spanish with fire ships. He sent burning ships into the port to burn the Spanish fleet and caused havoc. The Spanish Commander Sidonia restored order, but after a nine hour battle the wind forced the Armada into the North Sea. It sailed around Scotland and on to Ireland, but half the fleet was lost in extreme weather conditions. Queen Elizabeth became a legend in her own lifetime as a result of the English victory. She lived for another fifteen years and it was left to her successor, James Stuart, to make peace with Spain.

Did You Know?
When Sir Francis Drake had given the order for the English fleet to set sail, he is said to have continued a game of 'boules' he was playing on Plymouth Hoe and said that the Spaniards had rudely interrupted!

Casualties of War
ENGLAND
Ships: Eight fireships.
Men: Probably half, 7-8,000 men, mostly after the campaign. Death caused by hunger, wounds and disease.

SPAIN
Ships: Over sixty ships, mainly due to storms.
Men: Probably half, 13,000 men or more. Death caused by disease, drowning or massacre in Ireland.

Tudor Ships

Cutaway view of a two-decker galleon

1 Bowsprit
2 Prow
3 Forecastle
4 Anchor Cable

5 Capstan
6 Cookhouse
7 Gun Deck
8 Pump
9 Whipstaff

10 Officer's Cabin
11 Poopdeck
12 Rudder
13 Hold
14 Ballast
15 Hull
16 Keel

A Spanish Galleon

*Sir Francis Drake
The Spanish called him 'El Draco', The Dragon.*

An English Galleon

Myths about the Armada

■ Sir Francis Drake was not in command of the English fleet, it was Lord Howard of Effingham.

■ The biggest ship was English, not Spanish - it was Frobisher's ship, the 'Triumph'.

■ The English had better guns which could fire more quickly, but they ran out of ammunition.

■ The English ended with 50 more ships than the Spanish during the main battles.

■ The English sank only one ship and captured two.

■ The Spanish lost half of their ships and men in the worst Autumn storms ever recorded.

Combat Rations

ENGLAND

Sunday, Tuesday, Thursday:
1lb biscuit, 1 gallon beer, 1lb beef, 4oz cheese, 2oz butter.
Wednesday, Friday, Saturday:
1lb biscuit, 1 gallon beer, a quarter of stockfish, or the eighth part of a ling, 4oz cheese, 2oz butter.
Monday:
1lb bacon, 1 pint peas, 4oz cheese, 2oz butter.

SPAIN

Daily:
1.5lbs biscuit, or 2lb fresh bread, 1 pint of wine, 3 pints water.
Sunday and Thursday: *Monday and Wednesday:*
6oz bacon and 2oz rice.   *6oz cheese, 3oz beans or chick peas.*
Wednesday, Friday and Saturday:
6oz fish or squid, or 5 sardines, 3oz beans or chick peas, 1.5oz oil and a quarter of a pint of vinegar.

The Renaissance

The Renaissance came to England in the reign of Henry VII. He invited Italian artists and scholars to his court. It was a revival inspired by the works of ancient Greek and Roman writers and philosophers, which started in Italy and spread throughout Europe.

A Revolution of Art and Ideas
The Tudor period was a time of poetry and music, especially the composition of Italian-style madrigals for groups of singers. England led the way in the writing of music for keyboard instruments and a lot of traditional church music was written at this time. At Hampton Court you can see a small portable keyboard, which belonged to Anne Boleyn. There was a rapid spread of new ideas, helped by the invention of the printing press. This was as much a revolution in communication as the internet and email in our modern world today.

William Shakespeare

William Shakespeare is the most famous English playwright. He was born in Stratford-upon-Avon, Warwickshire in 1564. He might have followed in his father's footsteps if his glove-making business had not collapsed. Not much is known about his early life, but we know he married Anne Hathaway in 1582 and had one daughter and twins, a boy and a girl. No one knows why he moved to London, but he made a living as a playwright and actor. His first poem was published in 1592 and in 1594 he became a leading member of an acting company. He soon prospered during the end part of Elizabeth I's reign. He wrote an amazing number of plays, sonnets and poems.

Today, his plays are performed all over the world and many have been made into films. The Globe Theatre in London, where many of his plays were performed, has been reconstructed as it would have looked in Tudor times.

> Perform a Tudor play based on one of the historical events in this book. You may have to do additional research to find out some of the things the main characters said or did. Create costumes and simple sets, or you could perform the play using puppets.

Holbein
Hans Holbein was Henry VIII's favourite painter and was a master of the Renaissance style of painting. He was born in Augsburg, Germany in 1497. He encountered the works of the Italian Renaissance painters during a trip to Italy. In the early part of his life he worked in Switzerland as a book illustrator, but when the work slowed down he looked for work in England and gained a reputation for portrait painting. His work caught Henry VIII's eye and the King appointed him as his official court painter. He painted some of the most famous portraits we have of Henry and his wives, as well as prominent Tudor nobles and royalty. He died in London of the plague in 1543.

The Reformation
When Henry VIII split from the Roman Catholic Church, this was not the beginning of the Reformation in England, as he still continued the traditions of the Catholic faith. It was his son Edward VI who encouraged the movement away from Catholicism towards the Protestant faith. The Reformation was started in Europe by a German monk called Martin Luther. He protested against certain practices and traditions of the Catholic Church, which he thought contradicted the teachings of the Bible. He did not want to start a new faith, but to reform the existing church. However, the Pope would not listen to his protests and only forty years later, half of Europe was Protestant. Due to advances in printing, Luther's writings and those of other reformers spread quickly. The Bible was now available to ordinary people in their own languages, not just Latin, so people could read and understand it for themselves.

Printing
Around 1440 an efficient method of printing using moveable lead type was perfected by Johann Gutenberg of Mainz, Germany. As a result, printing presses appeared in every major city and cheap, mass produced books were available to a far greater number of people. Education was no longer just for the clergy and the wealthy. The first lead letters were copies of the monk's Medieval style of writing, but during the Renaissance period Roman letter forms were used.

Fashion

The clothes of the wealthy were studded with precious stones. Men wore embroidered jackets, fur-lined robes and short, padded trousers called breeches. They carried daggers which they used for eating, as well as swords. Rich women had skirts with frames underneath to make them wider. Some ladies wore the 'gabled hood' (see page 6). Men and women wore ruffs, or starched collars around their necks, unless they were poor.

The children in this picture come from a wealthy family, but all children dressed the same way as adults. Rich girls were forced into tight corsets reinforced with iron and whalebone to shape their bodies. This sometimes gave them broken ribs and stopped their lungs growing properly.

The Age of Discovery

The Portuguese sailed around the coast of Africa in search of gold, slaves and spices in Asia. The Spaniards sailed west to find an alternative route to Asia, accidentally discovering the American continent in 1492. The English wanted to find a northern route.

The Italian Christopher Columbus had already come to Henry VII to ask him to sponsor his voyage of discovery, but Henry turned him down. So, he went to King Ferdinand and Queen Isabella of Spain, who benefited greatly from his voyages. Five years later Henry agreed to fund another Italian explorer, Giovanni Caboto, who was based in Bristol. We know him as John Cabot. He sailed from Bristol in a small ship, the 'Mathew', with a crew of eighteen men in 1497. He was inspired by 100 year old tales from the explorer Marco Polo who spoke of the wonders of China.

Cod or Spices?

After a seven week voyage he discovered the Canadian coast, but Cabot thought it was China! In England he was welcomed back and the King awarded him an annual pension of £20. Cabot said that there were large amounts of cod, but Bristol merchants were more interested in spices from Asia. So, he told Henry that he would discover a new route to Asia for the spice trade and was given five ships and 200 men. In 1498 he set sail with items to trade with, but he never reached China and did not return home. The next King, Henry VIII, was not interested in discovering a north-west passage to China, so expeditions stopped.

Sir Francis Drake, a Pirate!

Drake first captained a ship at the age of 23. He sailed with John Hawkins to Spanish lands in Central America and the West Indies. The expedition was a disaster and they were captured, but managed to escape. Drake returned later to plunder more Spanish ships and lands and when he returned to England in 1573, he was a very rich man. In 1578 he became the first Englishman to sail around the world in his ship the 'Pelican', later called the 'Golden Hind'. On this voyage he continued to steal from the Spanish with the backing of Queen Elizabeth. He was basically a pirate! When he returned he was knighted. In 1596 he went on another voyage to the Caribbean, but he died of dysentery on his ship and was buried at sea.

Sir Walter Raleigh

Walter Raleigh was a favourite of the Queen. There is a story that on one occasion he removed his coat and put it over a large puddle, so that Elizabeth could walk over it. He was handsome, witty and well mannered.

The Spanish were already in South and Central America and the Queen wanted trading posts in North America, so that merchants could bring wealth back to England. Raleigh tried to colonise North America and he wanted to call the new land 'Virginia' after Elizabeth, the 'Virgin Queen'. The colony was unsuccessful, but he did bring back the potato and tobacco.

Raleigh became Captain of the Queen's Bodyguard and lived very well. The pearls on his shoes were said to be worth £6,000! Raleigh knew he could not marry the Queen, so instead he married one of her ladies-in-waiting. Elizabeth was furious and banned them both from court. He was not popular with the next King, James I, who put him in prison and eventually executed him.

Life at Sea

Not all men willingly became sailors and some were 'pressed' into service by press gangs who forcefully recruited them. Discipline was harsh and sailors were whipped for disobedience. Life at sea was very risky. You could get lost, shipwrecked or die of starvation or disease. More sailors became ill from food than died in sea battles!

Crews frequently suffered from scurvy because of their diet of salted meat and hard biscuits. They did not have fresh food, such as fruit or vegetables. The food was often eaten by rats, or infested with weevils. Life could be boring, with sailors spending several months at sea. They often passed the time dancing to fiddle music when they weren't making repairs to their ships.

Conquest & Expansion

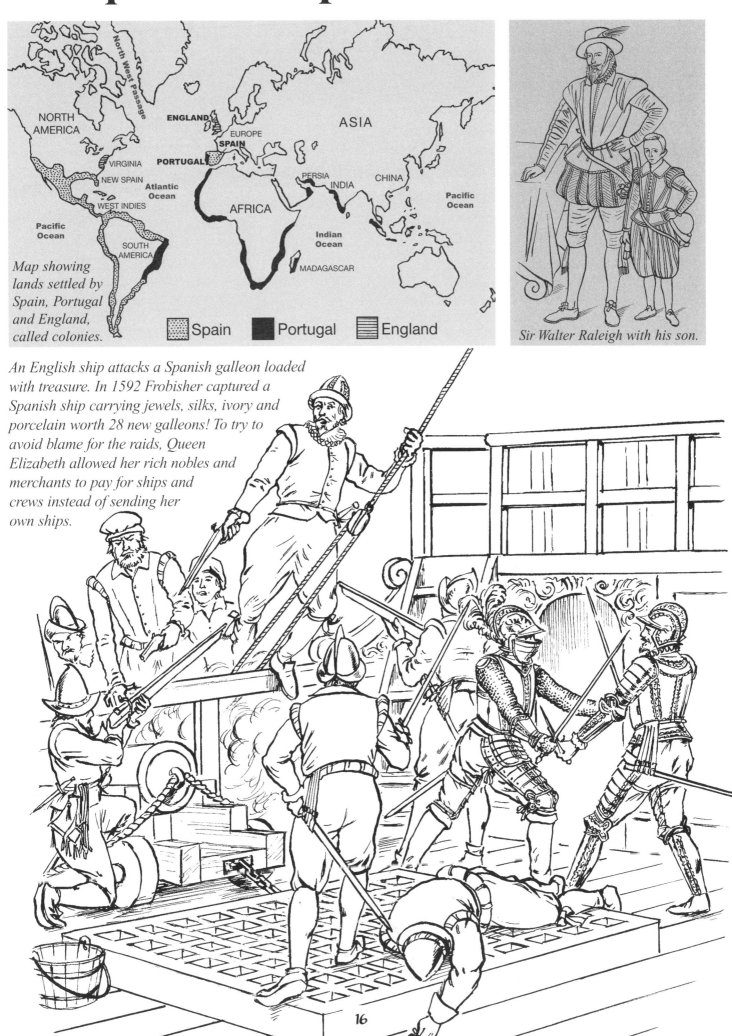

Map showing lands settled by Spain, Portugal and England, called colonies.

Spain   Portugal   England

Sir Walter Raleigh with his son.

An English ship attacks a Spanish galleon loaded with treasure. In 1592 Frobisher captured a Spanish ship carrying jewels, silks, ivory and porcelain worth 28 new galleons! To try to avoid blame for the raids, Queen Elizabeth allowed her rich nobles and merchants to pay for ships and crews instead of sending her own ships.

The Rich and the Poor

England did not have slaves, but by far the largest majority of people living in England were poor and they had no say about how the country was governed. Above the poor were the 'yeomen' class who owned some land, then 'gentlemen' and finally the wealthy nobles.

The Poor

These were labourers and crafts people, such as poor farm workers, tailors, shoemakers, carpenters, bricklayers and miners. In the towns they might live in shacks behind rich merchants houses. In the country they would construct hovels out of mud and branches, or make a wooden frame and build walls from wattle and daub. Those who could not find work in the towns and cities often became criminals, or beggars. Living conditions in a city like London were awful, without baths or toilets and diseases spread rapidly. Water from wells and pumps was sold by carriers.

'Poor Laws'

Laws were passed to make the rich give handouts to the poor. Other 'Poor Laws' tried to help travelling beggars get work, although they could be whipped if caught begging without a good excuse. Some wealthy people built houses for the poor, called 'almshouses'. Criminal behaviour was discouraged with public executions.

The Gentry

Tudor people were taught that God had ordered society in such a way that if people tried to rebel God would be displeased, so they largely accepted their lot. They called it the 'Great Chain', with God at the top and lifeless objects at the bottom. If you were clever and made enough money, you could rise up in society and become a gentleman. For no more than the cost of a nice house, you could buy a 'certificate of gentility' and obtain a coat of arms. Then you could have it put on your furniture, windows or clothes.

The Nobles

The rich liked to show off their wealth by building beautiful houses or building extensions. Cardinal Thomas Wolsey built a huge palace at Hampton Court on the River Thames, which was bigger than anything that the King had. To try and gain favour Wolsey gave it to Henry VIII. It had 280 guest rooms, but the King made it larger still!

Rich farmers, wealthy merchants and country gentlemen all built magnificent homes. The larger houses had to be big enough to entertain royalty. They would include a highly decorated 'great chamber', where visitors were received and plays could be staged. There might also be a 'long gallery' where paintings were hung, like the one at Hever Castle in Kent. Beds were decorated with tapestries or hanging silks and some floors had carpets.

Women

The Tudor period was dominated by men, and women were not thought responsible enough to have a career. However, three Tudor monarchs were women, although the Scottish churchman John Knox described this as 'monstriferous'! Tudor wives often worked very hard, looking after the children and animals, making food and earning extra money by turning wool into cloth. In the countryside they worked alongside their husbands at harvest time. Some made money by brewing beer and cider and selling it in their homes, which were called 'alehouses'. Many nobles spent a lot of their time at court, or abroad serving the king or queen and their wives ran their country estates for them.

Children

Rich Tudor parents preferred to have boys, so that they had a male heir to pass the family fortune to and to continue the family name. Rich mothers sent their babies away for up to eighteen months to be looked after by a 'wet nurse'. This person breast-fed and looked after the baby. In those days there was no substitute milk. Boys from wealthy families went to boarding schools, or other homes where they were shown how to behave in court. They may then go on to a university. Girls were taught the 'social graces' like music, painting, dancing and needlework. Boys were sent away to become 'apprentices' in order to learn a trade. So, many Tudor children spent very little time with their families. Even poor people like labourers sent their children away to become farm or house servants.

Tudor Homes

Yeomans House

A cutaway illustration of a yeoman's house. It is timber framed with wattle and daub. The hall was the main living room where eating, entertaining and cooking was done. Guests and servants slept here on straw mattresses.

The parlour was the most comfortable room and it was reserved for the family, as was the bedroom, or parlour chamber above it.

Food was prepared and goods stored in the service rooms.

A view from the River Thames of Hampton Court Palace, as it would have looked during the reign of Edward VI

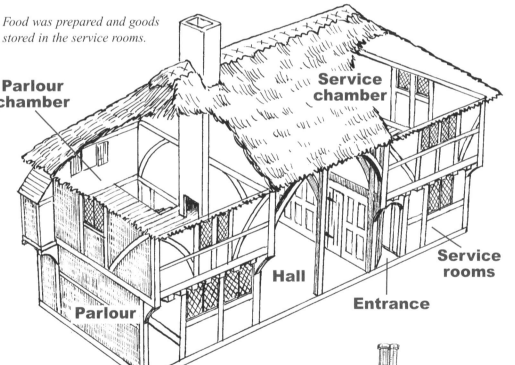

Parlour chamber

Service chamber

Hall

Service rooms

Entrance

Parlour

A Tudor lavatory or 'draught' which stuck out from the bedroom wall and emptied into an ash-filled pit below. There was no toilet paper, so people used leaves, grass, or little squares of old rag

Hanging Babies

Tudor babies were wrapped tightly in cloth because it was believed that 'the tender limbs of a child may easily and soon bow and bend and take various shapes.' Swaddled babies were also kept out of harms way by being hung from a wall peg!

A large country house owned by a wealthy family. It was built largely in brick, but some houses were built from local stone. In Tudor times most people lived in the country

Life & Death

Death was a common part of life in Tudor times. Many babies died and people did not live as long as they do now. Even though they had fresh air they often died of diseases due to poor sanitation or diet.

Food for the Rich

Food was an important part of life for the wealthy. When Elizabeth I visited Lord North, in three days the Queen and her court ate 67 sheep, 34 pigs, 20 deer, 1,563 chickens, 33 geese, 6 turkeys, 237 dozen pigeons, fish and wild birds, a cart load and two horse loads of oysters, 2,500 eggs and 430lbs of butter! Beer, or French wine was the usual drink of the rich. They also liked sweets made from marzipan coloured with vegetable dye and shaped into models of ships, castles, fruits, flowers or animals.

Food for the Poor

Vegetables were not eaten much by the rich as they preferred meat, but the poor could not afford meat. They ate bread made from barley, thin porridge made from oats and drank watered-down beer. They drank milk, ate cheese, lard and any vegetables and herbs they grew.

Entertainment

Tudor people did not have holidays, instead they had 'holy days', which were special church days when they had time off work, but by law they had to attend church. There were also twelve days of festivals from Christmas Day to the 6th January. Many people enjoyed watching plays, as it was only a penny to gain admission to a theatre like the Globe in London. They could visit a zoo to see lions, a tiger and a porcupine. Sometimes Tudor monarchs put on lavish shows and pageants which their subjects could watch. Henry VIII staged a mock battle on the Thames between the King's men and the pope's men. The pope's men were all thrown overboard! Other entertainment included watching public executions, which children could watch. People played a very rough version of football, which caused serious injury to the players and many enjoyed cruel sports such as cock fighting.

Tudor doctors wore strange protective costumes against the plague, because they believed the disease was carried in the air. Their long beaks were filled with oil and dried blood and ground-up toads were worn at the waist. They doused themselves with vinegar and chewed a plant called angelica before approaching a victim. They thought that all of this would protect them!

Wealthy Pastimes

The wealthy liked to watch 'masques' which were a kind of pantomime in their large houses. They might also enjoy 'falconry'. Special birds called hawks were trained to catch small animals and bring them back to their master. Henry VIII's palace at Whitehall had a built-in leisure centre. It contained tennis courts, a 'cockpit' for cock fighting, a bowling alley and a tilting yard. Tilting was jousting, but the riders were prevented from colliding by a fence, the 'tilt' and the idea was to score points against your opponent, not to kill them. You can see many of Henry VIII's jousting armours at the Royal Armouries in Leeds. Women liked embroidery, card and board games, such as chess, backgammon and 'shove groat'. They enjoyed gambling and in one year Henry VIII lost £3,500!

Staying Alive

In 1563, 17,404 Londoners died of the plague, which was one person in every six who lived in London at the time. Doctors thought the disease was carried in the air, rather than by bites from rat fleas. They thought many illnesses were caused by 'bad blood' and treated patients by cutting them, or sticking blood-sucking leeches on their skin! People went to 'apothecaries' to buy medicines, which were often made from odd ingredients like spiders webs, woodlice and mice! Poorer people used strange folk cures based on the fact that something resembled the illness. So passing someone over a donkey was supposed to cure a cough because the donkey's 'hee-haw' sounded like a cough! Walnuts were thought to be good for the brain and mental diseases because they looked like brains! Villagers could visit a 'cunning' man, or woman, who for a small fee, would give them magic cures for their illnesses.

Entertainment

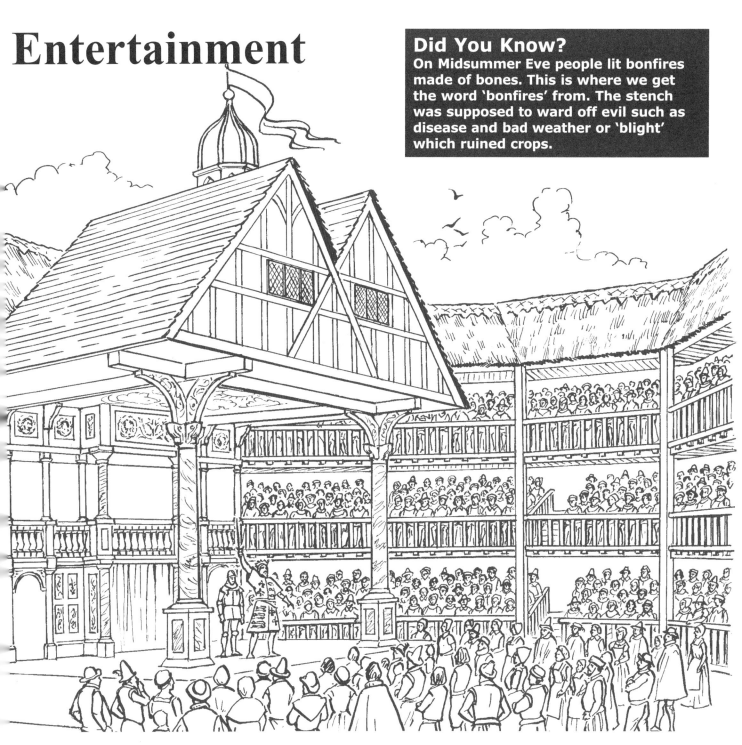

The illustration above shows the Globe theatre as it might have looked. James Burbage built England's first theatre, but when he died his sons Richard and Cuthbert dismantled it and hauled it across the frozen River Thames. They rebuilt it and called it the Globe.

Jousting in full armour was only for kings and nobles, but wealthy gentlemen could enjoy tilting. Here a rider is aiming to force the ring onto the end of his lance. The 'quintain', here shaped like a Turk, was to be charged at with the lance.

Tennis was not played on a lawn until the 19th century. Tudor, or 'real', or 'royal' tennis came from a French game which was played using a castle wall.

20

Giant Tudor Word Search

B	A	H	G	I	E	L	A	R	R	E	T	L	A	W	R	I	S	O	P
A	N	N	E	B	O	L	E	Y	N	S	T	O	W	O	H	E	Q	S	R
T	N	H	E	N	R	Y	V	I	I	I	D	N	M	Y	K	U	E	H	I
T	E	U	B	E	U	O	L	R	A	V	O	A	A	A	E	R	U	N	N
L	O	A	S	E	U	Q	S	A	M	D	R	I	R	E	A	R	D	O	C
E	F	L	A	C	T	U	S	N	N	Z	U	D	N	E	C	A	R	G	E
O	C	S	D	N	A	N	X	O	I	R	S	E	P	I	J	P	E	A	S
F	L	U	A	M	S	V	L	P	T	I	L	S	L	A	T	E	N	R	I
B	E	T	M	N	G	F	A	N	C	I	E	O	N	H	O	N	A	A	N
O	V	T	R	D	O	N	A	N	Z	K	H	E	E	P	C	I	I	F	T
S	E	O	A	R	A	T	A	A	A	T	S	G	I	I	A	R	S	O	H
W	S	N	E	E	S	R	B	H	A	E	L	S	R	O	S	E	S	E	E
O	A	W	H	E	F	E	S	C	Y	O	Q	P	T	M	O	H	A	N	T
R	O	O	T	R	T	M	A	M	B	L	D	S	S	R	L	T	N	I	O
T	D	O	I	H	A	M	O	E	O	O	E	C	E	E	Y	A	C	R	W
H	R	S	K	I	O	U	T	U	D	O	R	B	I	S	U	C	E	E	E
P	U	I	L	A	R	H	A	M	P	T	O	N	C	O	U	R	T	H	R
N	B	L	O	O	D	Y	M	A	R	Y	H	A	N	E	S	L	S	T	N
I	I	S	S	C	D	R	A	W	O	H	E	N	I	R	E	H	T	A	C
W	E	S	T	M	I	N	S	T	E	R	A	B	B	E	Y	U	T	C	Z

Battle of Bosworth	Bloody Mary	The Armada	Catholic	Marzipan
Queen Elizabeth	Princes in the Tower	Sir Francis Drake	Sir Walter Raleigh	Catherine Parr
Westminster Abbey	Protestant	Catherine Howard	Jane Seymour	The Globe
Tower of London	Anne Boleyn	Renaissance	Tudor	Anne of Cleves
Henry VIII	Catherine of Aragon	William Shakespeare	Hampton Court	Masques